The Journey

The Journey

Tips and Tales

Steve Gregory

Copyright © 2011 by Steve Gregory.

Library of Congress Control Number: 2011906614
ISBN: Hardcover   978-1-4628-6046-3
               Softcover   978-1-4628-6045-6
               Ebook   978-1-4628-6047-0

All rights reserved. No part of this book may be reproduced or transmitted in any form or by any means, electronic or mechanical, including photocopying, recording, or by any information storage and retrieval system, without permission in writing from the copyright owner.

This book was printed in the United States of America.

To order additional copies of this book, contact:
Xlibris Corporation
1-888-795-4274
www.Xlibris.com
Orders@Xlibris.com
98381

I have just completed reading your story . . . it is very interesting with a lot of good information. You make some very good points in your tips, particularly on having an asset based evaluation as opposed to highlighting all the deficits.

Your frequent frenetic, factual executive functioning episodes are interesting. I particularly like the part on planning. This is something that I talk about a lot with clients, as it really is the key to having a smooth day

Paula Hilborn, B.Sc.OT Reg. (Ont.)
Occupational Therapist

In this very personal journal, Steve recounts his experiences with Brain Injuryfollowing a car crash, and clearly illustrates how his life was suddenly and dramatically changed by his injury. However, it is not a story of a man who has been beaten by a fate that has dealt him a devastating blow. Like many others, Steve has picked himself up and worked to shape a post-injury life that will not be the same as the life that he might have had if the car crash hadn't occured, but a life that will see him productive and fulfilled in new ways.

John Kumpf
Past Executive Director, OBIA

Steve's book is a unique view into the world of acquired brain injury as seen from the inside. His idea of self-directed "frequent, frenetic factual executive functioning episodes" points to the limitless opportunities to focus on recovery outside of rehab appointments.

Steve has talked about this book as another step on his personal journey; hopefully it will inspire and empower other brain injury survivors as they undertake their own.

Marnie Russell
Service Coordinator
Community Head Injury Resource

"I have known Steve Gregory for a number of years with his community contributions and volunteering with the Brain Injury Association of Toronto and in the past 5 years with the Brain Injury Society of Toronto. For families and survivors this personal tale demonstrates Steve's incredible resilience, determination to succeed, commitment to rehabilitation and effective strategies which will assist people to ensure they "never give up" just as Steve never gave up. This is a powerful and meaningful personal story that will help and encourage many families and individuals to succeed despite extreme adversity and changes to their lives. Thank you for sharing your journey with us Steve and providing recommendations and strategies for success!

Colleen Boyce
Executive Director
NRIO

Table of Contents

Coma and Rehabilitation 11
Growing Up 15
Body
    Preamble 22
    Objective 22
    Evaluation 23
    Introspection 23
    Will 23
    Security 23
    Insight 24
    Exercise 24
    Control 24
    Demeanor 25
    Relationships 25
    Flexibility 25
    Dignity 26
    Self Image 26
    Self Talk 26
    Timing 27
    Media 27
    Self-Prompting 27
    Peace 28
    Service 28
    Frequent: of Frequent, Frenetic, Factual, Executive Functioning Episodes 29
    Frenetic: of Frequent, Frenetic, Factual, Executive Functioning Episodes 29
    Factual: of Frequent, Frenetic, Factual, Executive Functioning Episodes 29
    Executive Functioning: of Frequent, Frenetic, Factual, Executive Functioning Episodes 30

  Episodes: of Frequent, Frenetic, Factual,
  Executive Functioning Episodes 33
  Suicide 33
  Writing 34
  Humor 34
Conclusion 34
  Appendix A: Crash Scene 37
  Appendix B: Glasgow Coma Scale 39
  Appendix C: Ranchos Los Amigos Scale 41
  Appendix D: Executive Functioning Graph 43

FOREWORD

What is life about? Much of the world says it is about money, power, and sex. This is adequate for most life situations; however, once an accident enters the picture, it brings with it so many other variables so as to make use of God a factor. So then the equation becomes money, power, sex, and God.

These four items will form the foundation for this book.

Thanks to all who helped me in rehabilitation, and continued to do so by editing this book.

COMA AND REHABILITATION

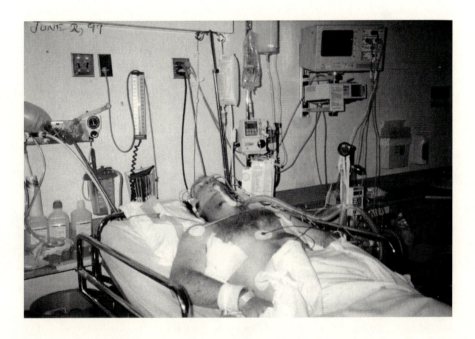

It was on the day of the major accident that I took money out of the bank to start my own business. At about 7pm on a road just outside of Gravenhurst on June 2, 1999, my truck veered off the road and went into a rockface. (see appendix A)

I was a 3 on the Glasgow Coma Scale (see appendix B) at the scene of the accident. I was in Intensive Care was moved to the hospital in Bracebridge for stabilization before shipment to Toronto. Some hours later it was raining and an airlift was out of the question, so I was transported the entire distance to Toronto (150km) via ambulance. I was brought to Sunnybrook and Women's College Hospital in northern Toronto.

Here I was a 4 on the Glasgow Coma Scale. At this point I was in Intensive Care at first. I remained in a coma for 2 weeks. At some point I had a tracheotomy performed. Here I stayed for another 4 weeks until I got an 8 on the Ranchos Los Amigos (see appendix C).

At this point I was transferred to Toronto Rehabilitation Institute (TRI). I was on the fourth floor here, in the head injury wing. I stayed here for about 6 months. I made some significant progress. I spent a lot of time on my bed thinking about my travels and generally daydreaming. It was here that I had my first Neuro-Psychological examination. Even at this stage I had some abstract reasoning at an average level for my age and education. A couple of firsts happened here. I wanted to be physically active and so running on a treadmill happened rather quickly. One day after some goal setting in which, one of my goals was to ride a bicycle again it happened in physiotherapy. There was a long hallway in the basement of the hospital. After a couple of trial sessions with the therapist holding on I was left to ride the bicycle on my own. This was a highlight of my week there. Initially, especially, the ride up to the fourth floor in the elevator was an adventure. My balance was so unstable at this point that I felt it necessary to hold on to the handrail while the elevator was starting off either ascending or descending. This remained for some time. At the present my balance has improved somewhat and I can now use stairs without absolutely requiring a hand rail, although this is still preferable. It was here that I received my first dose of therapy. Pretty soon the therapy support workers were coming to take me out. At one point I told my mom that I was tired of being a tourist. One part of these therapy support workers chores was to do laundry with me. We would then go back to the ward and play cribbage. The woman that I did this with and I had a running bet that the loser would buy the winner a brownie at the local convenience store. We had a good time doing this, I usually won, I think because she knew I liked brownies from this place. She would often take me to my parents place on the weekend also. The hospital is no place to stay on the weekend.

From TRI I was discharged to a residential setting, the now defunct Maynard place. Additional significant things happened here. At first the whole earth would tilt in my vision as I was walking along and when I would continue on as my body sensed the earth was flat. I started running here and would stop when I got dizzy. The dizziness is not vertigo nor is it BMP (Bone Morphogenetic Protein) both of which have been checked specifically at various points. I also was instructed to perform the Brandt exercises here and did so regularly until about 6 months had passed and I had seen Dr. Rutga (a specialist). It was during my time here that I underwent my second Neuro-Psychological test. Things had improved markedly, I was now hearing my own speech and so could compensate better for the slurring.

I left Maynard place and moved into my brother's house in the Beaches area in Toronto. At first, while here I would go to Variety Village, where I went while at Maynard place. They have an indoor track there so I tried running again, my dizziness would come and go, and get better and worse. I was given an examination by Dr. Rutga, which determined that my dizziness was not an inner ear problem. Even then there was a lack of information. However, I really desired to return to running. During my time immediately afterwards, I was given a time to go to a lawyer's assessment of my cognitive functioning. Here also I started cooking as therapy. I would heartily recommend it to any one. It helps with so many executive functions such as multi-tasking, organizing, planning and memory. I had my first experience with cooking while at TRI. It was near Christmas time and so when the OT asked me what to cook for a treat I immediately came up with Neopolitan Squares—a family favourite. Later while at my brother's house I started cooking meals. Often they involved some sort of pasta and fried chicken. The time cooking with Ellie became a highlight of my week.

About 3 years after the accident I had progressed far enough to allow me the opportunity for a job trial back at my previous employer. By this time I had finished with speech therapy. It was just going to be a monitoring time now. My speech has a definite nasal twang to it and there is a bit of slurring in it, however, it is perfectly understandable to a person who is listening. The technical term for this is dysarthic speech. Here I started on the treadmill in the gym again with some success although I still felt the need to always hold on to the frame. The job trial ended due to some vision problem with reading a book and I came back to Toronto. At this point my return to work rehabilitation effectively ended.. I tried running again and the dizziness was manageable so I ran in spite of it. Also I was hooked up with the Achilles track club and ran with them fairly often. Some time later the dizziness left and all that remained was a feeling of not being coordinated. This was about 38 months after the accident. That fall I decided to run in the Terry Fox Run, a 10k. It had been a goal to participate for some time. I then ran vigorously over the winter and my thinking started to improve. There were no tests done at this stage to determine this, however, daily tasks were improving. The insurance side of the accident performed the last testing. It was very superficial, and relied a lot on my vision, with which I was having difficulty. Sometime after the 4-year mark something happened to me that made my balance worse after running. In retrospect this was the fact that I had moved on in my thinking and now was concerned with my business as is mentioned later.

On exactly the fourth anniversary of the accident an arbitration hearing was organized to try and settle my case. This was done and the case was successfully closed on the fourth anniversary.

I heard from God one day and decided to start my own business with an idea that turned out to have been abandoned years earlier. However, I was motivated and pursued it until the business started to evolve and bring into play the Darrieus water current turbine. I started on this turbine while at General Electric Company (GE) and continued with it alongside my other jobs. At one point I was on contract to Natural Resources Canada. I made two that I sold while working at my last job and one is presently working. This business has allowed me to use my restored faculties in an area, which interests me. There are a number of Appendices attached. The most prominent being the new test results of my cognitive capabilities. You will note the high values of the abstract reasoning tests as well as the verbal memory tests. A combination of both of these is most unusual. As my lawyer told me, a person with a Glasgow Coma Scale of 3 is usually happy having breakfast. There are exceptions; however, they are just that, and not the norm.

GROWING UP

There was a local rural school, Castlemore, to which the majority of the students were bussed. I went there for kindergarten. My father had lobbied for starting kindergarten at this school and so it started before I required it. It was back to this school in Canada after a stay in Germany took up grades 1 and 2. My father was a teacher and he decided to go overseas to teach on a Canadian Forces based in Soest, West Germany. These years were marked by lots of travel and few forays on my own due to my age. During the last year in Castlemore, I started doing something, which I would later come to enjoy and later still use as a therapy tool, running. I had trouble reading the board in Grade 6 and was prescribed glasses. The student's council for this small school was also an activity which I joined in, events consisted primarily of hot dog sales and buying the teachers gag presents for Christmas.

Grade 7 was spent in England going to an English secondary school. My father was on another foreign teaching assignment, this time, on an exchange to England. Rugby was started here in it's homeland. I played rugby for gym for the first time, and did not enjoy it because of the position to which, I was assigned. I was asked to play second row—a position in the scrum, and this hurt my ears, making me not like the sport. Grade 8 was spent in Brampton going to a Senior Public School. This was the first year that my family started going to a new church, which, had a lot of things for young people going on. My involvement was minimal, however, it would, grow with time.

There was a staggered school start the first year at Chinguacousy, the local high school, and all the bus kids were on the early start. This meant that I had to get up early each day in order to catch the bus at 7:15. The first year went smoothly and I decided to play rugby in Brampton and the Midget 7's went to the provincial championships. They lost in the consolation final. In the second year the new school opened and so there was not a staggered start any more. The year started with a bang as I tried out for football. I did not make the cut, as an Interior Linebacker. This was the year I won a third place in the 9 to 11 math contest put on by the University of Waterloo where I would later attend. I decided to take music this year and played the trumpet. Playing rugby again I had a greenstick fracture in the shin one game early in the season, so sadly, I sat out the rest of the season.

In Grade 11, I started as an Offensive Guard on the football team. It was a small team since I was playing this position. Another season in rugby also came and went. I took music for the second time, however, I quit the course because I found it frustrating to spend so much time and not see any high marks.

Grade 12 meant it was time to study and I did not play football any longer, however, the rugby team went on a tour of Wales that year. I played Flanker on the seconds team. The team played 4 games and won one of these. Back to Brampton where I was the starter on the Senior team for Flanker. They progressed to the Ontario's and lost in the opening round robin to the eventual winner and the previous year's winner. Rugby was now fun for me. For the senior team this year, I earned the MVP. At the provincials I caught the eye of a coach for the provincial team and was asked to try out. I did not go to the try out as I was working for the summer at a Christian Service Brigade camp, where, for this summer I was Maintenance Captain. I had worked at this camp for the previous 2 years in a variety of positions, including, canoe instructor. This led to building my own cedar strip canoe.

Graduating from high school was not such a big thing for me as I always knew there was more school to come. This first year in University I roomed with a guy who was from the rugby team. We got along the whole year, mostly, I was studying. Then it was off for the summer and home to work at a moving company in downtown Toronto on my first co-op placement.

Then it was back to school for a third term and a basement apartment where I studied a lot of the time. Next it was home for another work term. This time I did testing as a Quality spot check person for a company making document processors.

Back to school in the summer, I spent it with a friend from the dorm first year and stayed in my ex-roommates house for the summer. It was during this term that I decided to go sky diving with a friend from high school. I went through the co-operative placement program again on campus and came away this time with a work term position. It was in the automotive industry, perhaps a foreshadowing of what was to come. The co-operative education system is good for many things, however, it is not good for relationship building, as you are always on the hunt for jobs and accommodation.

I went back to school, and did another work term in the automotive sector. After another term at school, next term I went through the interview process for job placement and was not matched with one. One morning at about 8:00am I received a call asking me to do a work term in Germany on a Canadian Forces base at Baden Solingen in West Germany. The decision was made to take it and I and a fellow co-op engineer left after Christmas but before New Years'. The trip was made safely and we arrived in Baden Solingen and went out for dinner with a friend of the work term group there. We sped over to France and had Tarte flambe that made such an impression on me that I later decided to cook them for one of my therapy sessions. I walked off base and went to Strasbourg for New Years' where I stayed in a Youth Hostel. I returned to Baden Baden and stayed in the Youth Hostel there also. One of the first outings I made with the work term crew was to buy a car. I looked at several and bought a small Fiat for transportation. I was away each weekend, but was sure to make it back to the base in time for the evening service at the chapel. At this point I bought some Telemark skis and tried to go skiing with them, however, I had limited success. Soon all the sightseeing was over and it was time to return to Canada. I did this and ended up staying in one of the Church colleges at the University arranged by my parents. At school, I started to specialize in heat transfer and fluids. For the first term of my fourth year I took a project which required me to work on a bearing system for large hydrogenerators. I then interviewed for and took a position with General Electric in Peterborough. The time there was enjoyable and I continued to perform the 5BX exercises (a Canadian regimen for fitness) for which I had acquired a book upon my return from Germany. I returned to school for the final term. I applied for some scholarships for my Master's and received several offers. The one I chose meant I was able to go anywhere in the province. Largely because of my involvement with my church in Brampton, I elected to go to the University of Toronto. At first I stayed in a dump until my brother and friends rented part of a house and invited me to join them. At the end of the school year I was looking for a place again and found one with a group of people near the Annex in Toronto. I continued to play rugby on the weekends with a club team near where I grew up.

One day, when everyone else was absent from the family farm, I decided to go dirt bike riding. I had gone down the driveway and come back up it at a fair speed. The growth that year of the branches had surprised me and I hit one of them which impacted one side of the handlebars and sent the bike swerving back and forth. After a couple of swerves I was stopped abruptly by running into a tree. At this point I was knocked unconscious for a period of time. As a result of the impact my glasses, which had earpieces which coiled round the ear flew out of my helmet. I was in this unconscious state some time before being awoken from this state naturally. When I did, I crawled forward and reached my glasses first. I promptly put them back on and removed my helmet. I then went back inside and called a friend to take me to the hospital. My knee was impacted and so I went to some physiotherapy for it. I went there and did some knee muscle tightening exercises, which solved the problem with my knee. I started running again afterwards and played rugby later on, though not regularly.

The remainder of my time at the University of Toronto went well. I continued to provide leadership at my home church for the cell groups of the college and career group. I suffered no cognitive setbacks from this accident and no noticeable effects until I was making the choice of which job offer to take. One was close to home and the other was in Peterborough. I elected to take the one in Peterborough, at least in part because of my paranoia with my leadership position in my home church. I was basically a loner, and so this paranoid state came easily to me. This was the first instance of paranoia in my work life and it was due to the motorcycle accident.

I started at General Electric Canada in the Edison Engineering program before I had defended my thesis in Toronto. This was an elite program for engineers that joined GE in order to groom them for future management positions.

Various jobs in the areas of manufacturing, design, and marketing were undertaken in the Hydro generator field in preparation for a long career there. The management there were taking good care of me. I participated in the various assignments over the course of the 2-year Edison program. These helped with my feelings of paranoia as they kept the assignments short—6 months max. each. Eventually the paranoia surfaced and I was writing notes to myself. Later I took to mailing these notes in registered letters to myself as I had heard that this was acceptable proof in a court of law.

Soon the notes became all consuming for me and I decided to leave GE in a very civilized manner with 2 weeks notice given. I left the job to start fixing up my house. I worked a lot on this house during the days that followed. I also started to work on the Darrieus turbine, which caught my interest while at GE. I continued to go to church even though I had changed churches while at GE because of my paranoia. I had gone to see several doctors and counselors while at GE because I knew something was wrong I received no real help.

The paranoia was at first just thoughts that would surface in my own mind. Later they became voices. This was a real problem that would plague me until after the coma accident when all my defenses were down.

My house renovations were nearing completion and so I then started back to work in the Toronto area at a job a University friend helped me get, since he was a supervisor there. The house was sold at a loss due to the fact that it had been purchased when the market was at its peak—subsequently it crashed.

The paranoia continued here, and soon, before the contract was up, I left to take another job in the area. I checked with a lawyer here, and this became the first of many forays into the legal field. I lived in the old family home in Brampton, which was now separated to allow my sister and family to stay there as well.

It was at this time that I started to talk to my uncle, who was a high school guidance counselor. These discussions led nowhere, I saw a Psychiatrist at the local hospital, this gentlemen, provided some help, though I was not stable long enough to get sufficient sessions with him to determine the medication and amount required. I was not a participant in the search for medication as my mind was driven by the paranoia. A job in Bracebridge for an automotive parts company was obtained and I traveled extensively and worked hard for them. I flew twice to Germany, once to Spain and twice to South Carolina. On several trips I was rushed to make the flights, however, on one notable occasion I arrived at the airport 15min before the flight was to take off. I made the flight barely. Later in Germany my paranoia was getting to me and I cut short this visit instead of going skiing in the Alps. I quit this job by throwing a seat adjuster on the desk and breaking my calculator in the process before storming out the door. Because of my paranoia I had lived at the family cottage for a period of time in spite of the 1.5 hr commute each way. The days were long as I typically worked from 8:15 to 7pm and then went home. Later during winter I lived in town and would work the same hours grab a paper, do the crossword and watch MASH.

I then got a job testing my Darrieus water current turbine in a river near Ottawa. I became paranoid at this job in spite of the freedom to move about and even took a tape recorder to work, however, the voices were too low on it to register. Some contacts would be made during my time testing that would later prove invaluable when I had my serious accident. I left this contract job also and took a contract job in the Toronto area in the automotive process equipment area. In the housing area, I moved back into the old family home which was now subdivided. I had the top floor, while my sister and her family had the main floor.. The paranoia surfaced here also as I took to insulating the floors as a result of the noise. I took another job after this contract one, as I was paranoid again and even went to the extent of buying phone cards so that I would not be heard at work.

I then received another job offer from a company in Huntsville, and proceeded to move to that area. This job was also boring at first, which meant I did not allow the paranoia to build up in me. After a year in this job when I would work 8:30 to 4:30 each day I was then promoted to the position of Program Manager. In this position I would look after several projects from concept to production. This was also in an automotive environment. I flew extensively for this job and kept my own schedule. With paranoia however, I worked very hard, often a 75-hour week. I had a dog at this point and the dog kept me company. I kept this up for some time until my paranoia got the better of me again. I quit this responsible job on short notice again, and was asked to return 2 weeks later. I did not, and no other people were involved in my life at this point. In fact I had asked my parents not to call me.

I did some odd jobs at this time, such as work on the fence of a boarding kennel, and some cement block work. There was no real meaningful contact with people at this time; I was also taking apart my computer. This would have been a very distressing period in my life if I was self-aware. As I was not and my paranoia ruled, I simply followed it and then was satisfied that I was living my life correctly. This fortunately changed after the accident when my level of paranoia had been forcibly reduced due to the accident and subsequent care by the medical staff. At first the Dr. increased the anti-psychotic dose twice to get me thinking clearly. This dosage was later increased as more healing occurred from the coma accident. Soon it was at the maximum to maintain an acceptable limit of side-effects. There is only one other anti-psychotic available that also has the side effect of seizures and possible death. After some discussion it was decided to stick with the current dose and medication, this is spite of lingering paranoia which raises its ugly head somewhat frequently when busy with people.

Some would say simply, that because of my unusual professional life I have developed a resilient spirit. I believe, however, that the spirit within me is that of the living God. My journey through this road of recovery has caused me to learn a lot. Some of these lessons are found in the following sections.

Preamble:

These episodes as I call them are to be of an ordered sense in their disorder.

As you wonder what to think about, I would suggest thinking of how things are made or manufactured as well as designed. Thinking about things related to feelings are not groundless, however, they are not well suited for the sort of thing we desire here. That is the promotion of an inquisitive self stimulating brain. This is the key to those long hours when you are by yourself and passing the time idly. The time waiting for meetings to start, the time for cabs to come, the time waiting for your computer to reboot, the time waiting for appointments all these times can be utilized to make your brain better. This is something the professionals are just figuring out now. Experience is a strict task master and so I would point to these exercises in order to effect positive change in rehabilitation. There is a quote that I think is appropriate here, it is by Mohammed Ali, "Champions aren't made in gyms. Champions are made from something they have deep inside them—a dream, a vision. They have to have the skill and the will. But the will must be stronger than the skill." This was given to me on a card with a picture of him on part, the quote on the other part with the inside handwritten by a person who appeared to be a friend as I was going through rehabilitation. However, the attitude changed when the professionals decided that I could not go back to work.

Philippians 1 4:8 comes to mind here—"Finally brethren, whatever is true, whatever is honorable, whatever is right, whatever is pure, whatever is lovely, whatever is of good repute, if there is any excellence and if anything worthy of praise, let your mind dwell on these things." Another pertinent verse here is Proverbs 23:7a "For as he thinks within himself, so he is." (NASB)

Objective:

To have a self-stimulating brain should be the initial goal of the thought patterns. This may be done simply with a driven, inquisitive, questioning mind that undertakes the compound directed initiation. That is that you can set a goal and pursue it without getting lost in the individual tasks—this is sometimes difficult for people without an injury.

Evaluation:

There is much made of the evaluation process within this rehabilitation complex. Evaluation is typically deficit based evaluation, i.e. what the survivor can no longer do. I propose a paradigm shift here to an asset based evaluation of the survivor. This provides the survivor with some dignity as they are in the midst of their recovery. A sense then that all is not lost would be facilitated thus providing a lower rate in suicides after the accidents.

Introspection:

This may be a natural for some survivors. Unfortunately, the accident itself has a tendency to promote disinhibition and so will make it harder than normal to do this. The thought here is to be reflective. At first, it will probably be of early life adventures. Later as some memory is restored it can move to recent events. Reflecting on the day's activities is beneficial to all. As a practice it can bring some real benefit to the one with the discipline to follow this pattern regularly. This also uses memory, thus improving it. Some method is needed in therapy for self-congratulation. There is little praise for the survivor as the days drag on. As small a thing as waiting for your watch to get to a even point, or for a digital watch, do not get noticed.

Will:

This term may also be called drive or initiation to make it more palatable to the professionals. It should really be called compound directed initiation. As the quote from Mohammed Ali says it is something that comes from within that is often affected by the injury.

Security:

This is a fundamentally important part of the mindset required for good rehabilitation. Failure to meet this requirement may result in anger and rage on the part of the survivor. How it is met will vary according to the emotional make-up of the individual involved. Most importantl is some assurance that their needs for the future will be met.

Insight:

This is a somewhat cryptic term at first to the survivor. There is much discussion of it but little explanation. This could be solved in part, by replacing it with the term self-awareness. This although not as short is a much more straightforward term for dealing with this circumstance. I believe what all survivors need is "limited insight" especially during the initial part of their rehabilitation. Enough to stay safe, however, enough to try things that are hard. This shows they have a drive inside and are motivated to try new things which are in fact old skills which they have lost due to the accident.

Exercise:

This is something that the professionals are aware of, however, encouragement is lacking

The two aspects are Cardio and strength. Cardio should be pursued as a matter of course, there are many types of cardio—vary it and set some goals. I think running is the best. You can think about some problems as you run, this helps you with multitasking. I used to pray for my nephew and niece when I was running—it was good for me and good for them. Achillies Track Clubs are around to help runners with disabilities—I highly recommend seeking a chapter out if there is one near you. Not only is the running good for you but the camaraderie helps as well.

Strength training is also useful. Do it regularly and try to develop to the point at which you are happy with your body. As you develop do more exercises in series so as to get a cardio effect from the weights. It is difficult. Remember, do what you can when you can do it.

Control:

This subject takes both the power and money aspects of rehabilitation. Different people for different items at different times are required for a successful rehabilitation. At first it may be that a powerful personality is needed other than the survivor. Later a more nurturing type of personality as the survivor seeks to find out what their cognitive assets are. It is difficult as the main party has an ever changing set of capabilities. Thus at first the professionals should be in charge. As time passes, this responsibility should shift to be out of their hands and more in the survivor's hands themselves. This will vary from case to case; however, ownership of the person's life is important for the person themselves and they should be given the rights to control their own destiny as much as possible.

Demeanor:

This is important also during your rehab and some things are not accepted at all times and by all people. A quote I read recently comes to mind, "Quiet minds cannot be perplexed or frightened but go on in fortune or misfortune at their own private pace, like a clock during a thunderstorm" by Robert Louis Stevenson. It is good to have a quiet demeanour during your rehab. Be self-assured though and learn which people you can trust—it may turn out that you can trust no-one but your self. Be very careful if you find yourself in this position. This was the position that I found myself in—it is very lonely.

Relationships:

This is a confusing situation in brain injury. All of a sudden you have all these people taking an interest in you. You have no control over who they are or what they do with you. There are many types of relationships in rehabilitation. Keep relaxed as you cannot control how others will react to you. Some relationships are there simply because they are being paid to do so. Others are paid but care and still others are not paid and care. There are a few people who will stick with you on your course of rehabilitation. Put some effort in and think about their needs also. Become concerned with other people than yourself. This is key in community re-integration. To have good friends you must be a good friend is often true.

Flexibility:

This is important after an accident. The old ways of doing things may no longer be viable. The survivor may not be able to do the same things the same way—look for another way of doing them. It may take longer or not be as tidy but in order to complete the same task one must adapt. Grocery shopping is one task. Previously, perhaps, one would just go shopping without any list or budget. Now these items become essential in completing the task successfully. Adapt to your new abilities.

Dignity:

This is a section of the rehabilitation that does not get covered elsewhere. Every human being deserves this and as a survivor you treasure dignity. So much of the decision making is done behind closed doors without the survivors having any input. If the person is involved in the decision making then no decision should be made behind closed doors. Rehabilitation should be a totally open process. Right now it is pervaded by the professionals' insecurity. This opinion is wholly from my own experience and should be taken with a grain of salt. The professionals believe in the model of rehabilitation that they prefer. It is where the professionals make all the decisions and are accountable to no-one.

Self Image:

This is really part of the bigger picture of dignity. Do you believe that there is a reason for you being given a second chance? Do you take your self-worth from what others say of you? There is a very real necessity here for a self-validation mechanism.

God can provide this missing link between lives lived in the past and a life that is experienced with all the joys and sorrows intended.

Self Talk:

What are the small attitudes that you have in your life now? Is there an asset based evaluation of your behavior and actions? This self talk is one of the most important attitudes that you are entrusted with. What you do with this energy is your choice. Do you choose an asset based evaluation of your condition or do you only look at the deficits. Be your own cheerleader. Remember, you are the only one on your side. So act accordingly.

Timing:

This is the all important issue really. The timing of when in your life the accident happened. The timing of availability of various rehabilitation facilities and people. Timing of the availability of job training, the economy and of course your own drive.

Procrastination is a factor here. "Never put off till tomorrow what you can do today." This is a famous saying—it should be well understood by all survivors who want to make a good recovery. Sitting around all day is not in anyone's best interest. Though this may be needed at times. Take everything with a grain of salt. There are no hard and fast rules for negotiating successfully the path of rehabilitation.

Media:

This is the all encompassing reality these days. It is everywhere and you can access it everywhere and any time. Be careful with all these avenues appealing to you for your time and energies. They may be entertaining for a time, however, how do they work out in the long term. In the initial days of the computer there was a phrase around GIGO (Garbage In, Garbage Out) this applies in our case. What you want to do with those spare moments is to think. Think for yourself. Think long and hard about things. Some things do not come easily. Make use of the spare time you have. Instead of filling it with the latest movies on TV or the latest tunes on your iPod try and fill your mind with good things such as are outlined in the Executive Functions section.

Self-Prompting:

This is the reverse of what can typically occur early in rehabilitation. Typically, the professionals will try and trigger a thought in you that you do not have the skills to do at this early stage of recovery. This activity when undertaken by some one other than yourself is called prompting. All of us need this at some point whether it is because we have a lot on our plate, we are getting older, or whether we had a brain injury. Self-Prompting requires one to keep this activity foremost in one's mind for a period of time. And therefore being able then to present the thought when it is needed.

I had a recent occasion when this failed for me as I had taken it for granted. I was headed off to the post office with a particular complaint. However, when I arrived at the desk and presented the piece of evidence the woman behind the counter assumed I was drunk because of my speech and unshaven condition and proceeded to tell me why everything was OK. I got out of there and realized that I had failed to lodge my complaint accurately. I was very disappointed in myself and resolved to self-prompt more vigorously next time. How often you must think of the particular thought will depend on your own memory. Once, I went to the grocery store without a list. While there I remembered only 4 items initially, but then proceeded to walk thru the store until I had picked up all the items on my mental list. I do not recommend this however. The best way to avoid buying things you do not need is to make a formal list and take it with you. If I had done this with the Post Office, I would not have been so disappointed with the results.

Peace:

This is a rarity during the initial days. Especially for your family where there is so many new things going on. When you first become aware you may be in a place where you in all likelihood do not want to be. There is much confusion. Train your mind to be at peace. This will facilitate the following abilities. Become aware of some meditation techniques, they are helpful in this process.

Service:

This topic will change as you go through rehabilitation. At first everyone will be at your service. Depending on your family, friends, and circumstances of your accident, they may be for the rest of your life. It is good though to turn the tables and serve others.

Do what you can when you can do it. Open the door for people, serve in a soup kitchen, give blood, serve on a board. Do something for others. This may be hard depending on the outcome of your accident.

These next 5 points are the most important of the book. They will enable you to make the most of your brain injury. Each case is different, give yourself some grace here.

Frequent: of Frequent, Frenetic, Factual, Executive Functioning Episodes

This is a function of the stage of the injury. At first it can be whenever you are free from therapy as it is more intensive at first. Later it can be exercised while doing something such as waiting for a bus or a phone call. Take care to be able to determine when you are exercising your brain and when you are making life decisions. The rapidity of the thought process should be performed in light of the consequences of the decision. Do not confuse how your mind works in spare moments with your life decision making process.

You should strive to have a train of thoughts going through your head. An example could be:

As you sit down you notice a plant. So you wonder where did I buy this plant, when was the last time I watered it, how old is the plant, are there new growth spurts and is it getting enough sun where it is?

Frenetic: of Frequent, Frenetic, Factual, Executive Functioning Episodes

Ideally it should happen as often as possible. At first your mind may tire easily of this and you may become bored with being forced to think about things that are constructive. As time passes step up the pace as this will get you ready to multitask at work.

Factual: of Frequent, Frenetic, Factual, Executive Functioning Episodes

Objective facts are the point of this directed thinking. This can be made open to aid as opposed to subjective feelings which are personal. Develop a hobby at some point. One of your interests you now have or perhaps one you had previously. Think about this and use your memory and reasoning to help you in the understanding of the situation of your chosen interest.

Executive Functioning: of Frequent, Frenetic, Factual, Executive Functioning Episodes

Often in survivors, this portion of the brain has suffered some damage and is the most apparent culprit in the inability of the survivor to think and reason in a manner which would allow them to return to competitive employment.

Analyze, Analyze, Analyze. Look at the world around you and find order in it. Talk with some people about how things are made and how they work. This will help you to understand the forces at work in nature and machinery. People's reactions are much harder to gauge. Practice with these also though as they will bring some predictability to your world. Optimize everything around you—the way you do your laundry, the way you cook your meals, the way you organize your day, and the patterns you see everyday in things such as the lowly digital numbers on the clock radio in your bedroom. For example:

7:07 is LOL upside down and backwards. There are many patterns to be recognized in the clock. Or better yet, look at the time of 7:34 and then synthesize the numbers 10:4 which is CB lingo for OK.

As you go through your day learn to optimize it before it happens. Play out the things you have to do during the day and strive to optimize their order and timing. Go running before you eat. Pick up the mail on return from buying the milk at the store. Analyze your day before it happens. For example, today I was thinking of what to have for dinner and decided on the two left over cannelloni in the fridge. Next question was how to reheat them. Decided to put them in the microwave, next decision was in which dish, Eventually I decided to leave them in the package they came in as the other dishes were starting to heat up and I could easily dump them from the package into the dish when hot. This will help connect the neurons in your head like nothing else. Do all these things tirelessly, it is your future at stake here after all.

Pick out patterns in pieces of fabric, in building design, in car design, in carpet patterns, in furniture, in stores, in regulations, in everything find patterns.

There are many TLA's in rehab.(three letter acronyms) Learn to analyze these and how to synthesize your own. TSW's and MSW's are two that you will see kicked around for sure.

Remember, Remember, Remember. While passing time endeavour to remember things from the previous day or week. A recent episode of this in my own life was prompted by a look at the sky. From this a similar color scheme was remembered from a classmates shirt in University and that led to a remembrance of a singer he liked which led to a floormate from first year and fellow classmate which led me to wonder whether I had picked up an album by this singer during my indulgence in music at which point I decided to abandon the train of thought. Relax and be patient with yourself. Things may not come right away, and there may be some keys to unlocking certain events details such as what happened that morning. Practice remembering what colour clothes you are wearing before looking at them or what you had at the various meals or snacks of the day.

Don't get angry or frustrated at yourself for not remembering something—remember you had a bad accident and now you must get on with what you can develop for yourself. Practice this often. As often as your drive permits. Celebrate the first time ghosting occurs. This is when you don't remember whether it was last time or the time before that it happened. This is progress.

Get in the habit of having several lists of things you need to get/buy during the week. At first always write down all the things you need to do in a list. Practice slowly bringing this process back into your head if and when you can. This is part of planning.

Plan, Plan, Plan. While daydreaming think of the days or weeks ahead and plan through them. Plan what you need to do before what and what you need to take with you. Make a list of all these things. Refer to your list as often as you need to. Jot some things down as they come to mind. This will ensure that your events will progress smoothly.

Buy a daytimer. Learn to use it even for the smallest items which will seem easy at first and a waste of time for writing them down. There are books on this. "The 7 habits of Highly Effective People" is one such book. I am a fan of the Franklin-Covey daytimer, which, if used effectively will become your new life. There are many aspects to a good daytimer—learn to use them even for the smallest things while you have the time. Using it then for the bigger things falls into place.

Plan your clothes and your meals—at first this may be done with the aid of writing them out. Try and progress to doing them just before. I know of one gentleman who has a list of his day's tasks that he takes with him each and every day. Now often when he looks at the sheet he sees that he is doing as he should. Try to plan "what if" scenarios. What if this happened then what would I do or what if that happened what would I do.

What you plan, remember and analyze should be geared to you. Pick topics that are pertinent to your life and situation. Plan your meals with the help as part of your therapy. Cooking is a great source of circumstances to help stimulate your brain. Plan not only what you will cook for each meal but how you will cook it. Will you put the pot on for pasta water before you start cutting the chicken to brown?

Plan tasks such as laundry. In your minds eye go through the steps of getting the clothes to the washer, putting the soap in starting the machine after setting the load size correctly as well as the wash cycle. Recently I was planning my day, at first I decided to eat at 4 as I had Skype date at 5 then a service person coming at 6. Such planning may not come easily. At first accomplishing one thing per week will be all you will be able to manage especially when you are in the hospital. Rehearsing these tasks prior to doing them will make them easier to do when the time comes and will help with the re-organization of your brain. Plan what you will wear for the events and people you will meet during the day. As you progress, writing them down for the intermediate steps may not be necessary. This is the goal, to have a mind that lets your executive be used in your free time without any written cues. This is what I have progressed to, the self-stimulating brain at work.

These three facets of your executive should form the basis for much of your activity during your idle times. Give yourself a pat on the back especially at first as you start to think this way. Most professionals have nothing to say about this. Some professionals are working only to make money then to get referrals then to feel good about themselves and finally to consider your needs.

And remember, "He who fails to plan plans to fail",

Do not get down on yourself if you do not remember something or fail to plan or reason for the optimum result. Remember you had an accident. Your life will never be the same. I, myself, am fully in the glass is half full camp and think that with that sort of thinking you can accomplish being the best you can be after your accident.

Develop a hobby to pass the time. There are many things online these days so if you have the use of a computer, develop some interest in groups there. Spend some time on your hobby, become a world class expert in that particular area.

Episodes: of Frequent, Frenetic, Factual, Executive Functioning Episodes

The timing of these forays into the use of the executive may also vary greatly, at first, perhaps three or four per hour. However, as you progress through your therapy a number like 20 might be more appropriate. This comes about by looking to your spirit for strength and being aggressive in your thought process alone.

Suicide:

Let's start by naming the topic. Everyone on the planet thinks about this but no one talks about it. Let's talk about the elephant in the room—everyone knows it's there but no one wishes to talk about it. After an accident, during the confusion you may think there is no point. This is where the professionals need to come in with the items listed above. Primarily the patient's dignity must be respected. There was a point when I needed some help, at the stage, where everyone was saying that I was useless. This is to their shame. They were not using an asset based evaluation of my skills and deficits as they should have. Indeed I think this is lacking in the industry today.

We, as survivors are sort of like the ostrich in Job 39. The ostrich here is cited as an example of God's abilities. We are unique in the human population. We have a unique contribution to make to society. It is your job to figure out what that is for you given your abilities and how to make it happen in your own life. We have some absurdities about us that are beyond reason. We should not consider suicide as an option for a response to what we have been given. DO NOT COMMIT SUICIDE.

Writing:

It may sound like a really effeminate thing to do, but putting your thoughts on paper and bringing them out into the open can do you a lot of good. Start small, just about your day and the events that happened. Reflect on your day and so use your memory. Plan your week and so use your executive. Talk about your feelings and your dreams, let them be written down instead of just floating around in your head. You should set aside a place to write and a book to write in as well as a time to do so.

Humor:

This is a must for anyone going through therapy of any kind. A quote comes to mind here; "A sense of humor can help you overlook the unattractive, tolerate the unpleasant, cope with the unexpected, and smile through the unbearable" this is from Moshe Waldoks. Develop your own sense of humor here. For my part one therapist said "I don't think you can blame your sense of humor on the accident." That in itself was a break from the drudgery of rehabilitation.

Conclusion:

This is the end. This is not how you thought your life would end up. No one plans an accident. Now, you must come to grips with the effects and move on. How you do this will determine to large extent your future success and happiness. Remember do not get distracted by the sheer number and volume of reports. Here is a quote that I think is appropriate here. "Vitality shows not only in the ability to persist, but in the ability to start over", F. Scott Fitzgerald.

The best anyone can determine, two factors are critical in determining the outcome. The pre-accident level of formal education and the activity level. As for myself I had both these on my side and so I have done well.

I would like to leave you with a quote from a cancer survivor which summarizes much of what I have been saying here with Bernadine Healy's six guidelines for recovery

By way of introduction, Bernadine Healy has run the American Red Cross and the National Institutes of Health. She wrote in the April 9th, 2007 issue of U.S. News & World Report about her recovery from cancer. Her professional experience hadn't prepared her to deal with a serious illness in her own life:

1) Control what you can.
2) Stay constructive.
3) Avoid the anger trap.
4) Look at the humor.
5) Insist on respect.
6) Nourish your spirit.

In conclusion: Never give up.

Never **Ever** give up

APPENDIX A:

Crash Scene

Courtesy of the Gravenhurst Banner

BAD ACCIDENT. Bracebridge OPP are still investigating this nasty looking accident on Bethune Drive at Industrial Drive in Gravenhurst last week. There was little information available about the accident except that the driver sustained severe injuries.
Photo by Andrew Wareing

APPENDIX B:

Glasgow Coma Scale

The **Glasgow Coma Scale** or **GCS**, sometimes also known as the **Glasgow Coma Score** is a neurological scale which aims to give a reliable, objective way of recording the conscious state of a person, for initial as well as continuing assessment. A patient is assessed against the criteria of the scale, and the resulting points give a patient score between 3 (indicating deep unconsciousness) and either 14 (original scale) or 15 (the more widely used modified or revised scale).

GCS was initially used to assess level of consciousness after head injury, and the scale is now used by first aid, EMS and doctors as being applicable to all acute medical and trauma patients. In hospital it is also used in chronic patient monitoring, in for instance, intensive care.

The scale was published in 1974 by Graham Teasdale and Bryan J. Jennett, professors of neurosurgery at the University of Glasgow. The pair went on to author the textbook *Management of Head Injuries* (FA Davis 1981, ISBN 0-8036-5019-1), a celebrated work in the field.

GLASGOW COMA SCALE

There are a few different systems that medical practioners use to diagnose the symptoms of Traumatic Brain Injury. This section discusses the Glasgow Coma Scale. is based on a 15 point scale for estimating and categorizing the outcomes of brain injury on the basis of overall social capability or dependence on others.

The test measures the motor response, verbal response and eye opening response with these values:

I. Motor Response

    6—Obeys commands fully
    5—Localizes to noxious stimuli
    4—Withdraws from noxious stimuli
    3—Abnormal flexion, i.e. decorticate posturing
    2—Extensor response, i.e. decerebrate posturing
    1—No response

II. Verbal Response

    5—Alert and Oriented
    4—Confused, yet coherent, speech
    3—Inappropriate words and jumbled phrases consisting of words
    2—Incomprehensible sounds
    1—No sounds

III. Eye Opening

    4—Spontaneous eye opening
    3—Eyes open to speech
    2—Eyes open to pain
    1—No eye opening
The final score is determined by adding the values of I+II+III.

APPENDIX C:

Ranchos Los Amigos Scale

There are a few different systems that medical practioners use to diagnose the symptoms of Traumatic Brain Injury. This section discusses the Ranchos Los Amigos Scale.

The Ranchos Los Amigos Scale measures the levels of awareness, cognition, behavior and interaction with the environment.

Ranchos Los Amigos Scale

Level I: No Response
Level II: Generalized Response
Level III: Localized Response
Level IV: Confused-agitated
Level V: Confused-inappropriate
Level VI: Confused-appropriate
Level VII: Automatic-appropriate
Level VIII: Purposeful-appropriate

APPENDIX D:

Executive Functioning Graph

Executive Functions

Measures of deductive reasoning, abstract reasoning, conceptualization, planning, novel problem solving, initiation, and mental flexibility.

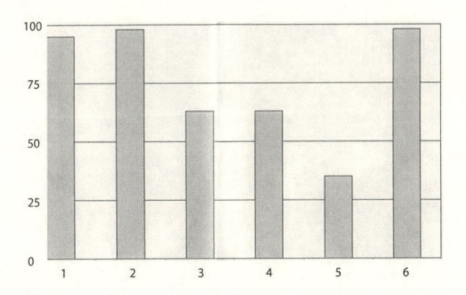

These tests were performed as part of the larger Neuropsychological exam. They show a return to my original state as best as can be determined given the error possible in any such testing.

Edwards Brothers, Inc.
Thorofare, NJ USA
June 6, 2011